MUNICIPAL BROADBAND:
A GUIDE TO POLITICS, POLICIES, AND SUCCESS FACTORS

By Matthew Howard

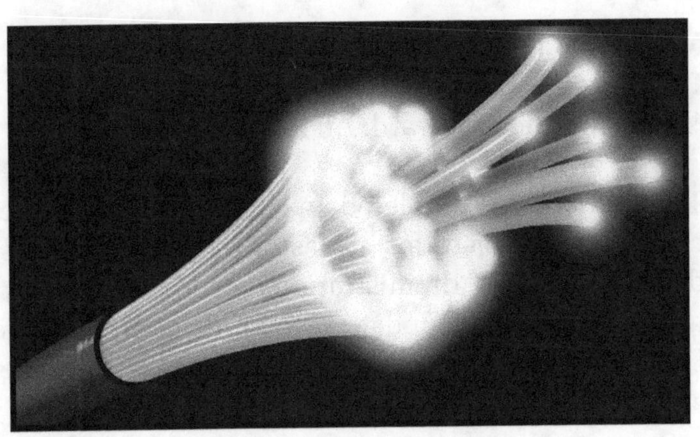

2017 Paperback Edition

ISBN-13: 978-1981969944
ISBN-10: 1981969942

"Municipalities typically have lower costs than private entities and do not seek the high short-term profits that shareholders and investors expect of private entities. As a result, municipalities can sometimes serve areas that private entities shun and can often provide more robust and less expensive services than private entities are willing to offer."

—James Baller, The Baller Herbst Law Group.
State Restrictions on Community Broadband Services or Other Public Communications Initiatives (as of June 1, 2014).

CONTENTS

PREFACE..7

I: INTRODUCTION...9

II: THE POLITICS OF MUNICIPAL BROADBAND............13
    1. Municipal Broadband Is Not a Partisan Issue.   13
    2. What Are the Restrictions, and Who Benefits?   15
    3. Municipal Broadband in Arizona.   19
    4. The FCC's Role.   23
    5. Competition and Public Utilities:
       A Philosophy for Broadband Policy.   25

III: SUCCESS FACTORS: POSITIVE RESULTS
FROM MUNICIPAL BROADBAND...............................33
    1. Lake County, FL.   33
    2. Danville, VA.   36
    3. Chanute, KS.   38
    4. Chattanooga, TN.   40
    5. Bristol, VA.   43

IV: FAIL FACTORS:
EVALUATING TERMINATED PROJECTS.......................45
    1. St. Cloud, FL.   46
    2. Philadelphia, PA.   47
    3. Tempe, AZ.   48
    4. LaGrange, GA.   52

V: MAKING IT HAPPEN: TECHNOLOGY, FINANCING,
AND BUSINESS MODELS...57
    1. Technology Infrastructure.   59
    2. Financing.   61
    3. Business Models.   63
    4. Summary.   65

VI: QUICK GUIDE TO SUCCESS
AND FAILURE FACTORS..65

VII: CONCLUSION 71

FOOT NOTES and REFERENCES 73

APPENDIX:
FIBER NETWORKS: AN ABBREVIATION GUIDE 82

MORE POLICY BOOKS FROM MATTHEW HOWARD 83

PREFACE

In December 2017, two months after I completed the original version of this book, FCC leadership voted 3–2 to undo net neutrality provisions of the 2015 Open Internet Order. Like millions of Americans, I was disappointed in this outcome. My previous essays on net neutrality were far from neutral. They clearly favored the 2015 Order as championed by former FCC Chairman Tom Wheeler.

The connection between net neutrality and municipal broadband may not, at first, be obvious. But deeper analysis reveals that private, corporate Internet Service Providers (ISPs) are the primary beneficiaries of repealing net neutrality policy. These companies are the same ones who spend millions of dollars campaigning against municipal broadband. From their perspective, lobbying state and federal legislatures makes good business sense, as does funding the campaigns of state and federal legislators, and dragging municipalities into court to endure costly litigation. These ISPs, which are well-known cable and telecommunications corporations, desire total control of Internet access in the United States, the freedom to monopolize the industry, and zero restraint in charging consumers for Internet service. The motive is age-old and predictable: profits.

When cities build their own broadband networks and take control out of the hands of private ISPs, this public action threatens private monopolization.

Private ISPs respond by lobbying state legislatures to enact laws restricting the growth of municipal broadband. In about half of the states in the nation, they have been successful. But a rising tide of hundreds of municipal networks resists the control of private ISPs, delivering more bandwidth and higher speeds at a lower cost than the corporate giants can (or want to) match.

Municipal broadband has become a crucial component of a free and open Internet. The FCC's leadership, comprised of political appointees, comes and goes with the current presidential administration, and Congress has shown no interest in revising the outdated Telecommunications Act of 1996 to properly classify and protect Internet access as a public utility. Municipal broadband networks offer a solution the federal government cannot or will not establish: publicly owned and controlled Internet access, on a local, grass-roots scale.

Writing about net neutrality and municipal broadband is challenging, because every day brings new headlines about the ever-shifting battle to free the American public from private control of the Internet. The history and current events are complex, but not incomprehensible. Municipal broadband networks are achievable in practical, profitable ways, and I hope this book contributes to their development.

I. INTRODUCTION.

Not all municipal broadband projects are created equal. Hundreds of these projects exist in the United States, and they abound in Europe and abroad. Municipal projects vary greatly in their local political environments, technology choices, financial planning, business models, monetization strategies, social goals, and relation to the private sector.

This diversity makes it difficult for local policy makers to draw firm conclusions about the viability of municipal broadband in their communities. For every wildly successful story, there seems to be a corresponding tale of failure. Some new projects enjoy widespread media coverage hailing them as the next great success, only to end in disappointment a few years later. Yet small towns across the nation create dramatic economic turnarounds which enjoy little fame beyond their local communities.

No public administrator wants to champion a project which fails to deliver, and the conflicting stories about municipal networks might make them seem like a gamble. But these projects do not rely on a random roll of the dice. Clear trends have emerged since the turn of the century, patterns of success and failure which repeat themselves in case studies by federal agencies, local administrators, academics, and grass-roots advocacy groups.

An examination of these documented cases results in guidelines administrators can use to plan and implement successful municipal broadband projects, and avoid the common pitfalls which lead to failure. These guidelines arise from comparing and contrasting what *has* worked with what *has not* worked in the past. They provide a strong foundation upon which municipalities can build robust, profitable networks to reduce governmental expenses and improve Internet service for residents, businesses, and public institutions.

When a municipality builds its own network and becomes its own Internet service provider (ISP), then Internet access becomes a public utility, much like other utilities such as water, electricity, waste disposal, and all the services we have come to see as basic to our modern standard of living. This shift lies at the heart of an ongoing political struggle at the state and federal levels, where Internet access has long been treated as a luxury service provided to customers by private companies.

No study of municipal broadband would be complete without an examination of this political dimension. At the state level, private cable companies and ISPs, along with their lobbies, write legislation which limits, hampers, or outright bans municipalities from building their own broadband infrastructures and offering Internet service as a utility. Through contributing to election campaigns, lobbying, and drafting legislation, these private companies exert incredible pressure on state legislatures to block local governments from meeting their own needs for improved Internet technology.

At the federal level, the Federal Communications

Commission (FCC) remains embroiled in an ongoing debate about whether to regulate broadband as a "common carrier" service—a public utility. The FCC's 2015 Open Internet Order reclassified broadband as a telecommunications service under the FCC's power to regulate. This move was consistent with the FCC's interpretation of its authority as granted by Title II of the Telecommunications Act of 1996, and consistent with recent Supreme Court decisions supporting the FCC's authority to make that interpretation (summarizing Howard, 2015).

But that reclassification spent all of 2017 under the threat of being undone by the FCC when newly elected President Trump appointed Ajit Pai to replace the 2015 Order's champion Chairman Tom Wheeler. As of October 2017, the 2015 Order remained in regulatory effect, but the fate of the Internet's status as a public utility at the federal level was uncertain. December 2017 saw this matter brought to a head when FCC leadership voted 3–2 to repeal key aspects of the Order's net neutrality provisions—the rules against blocking, throttling, and paid prioritization—and remove the Title II classification of broadband as a common carrier service.

While successful municipal broadband projects were planned, implemented, and established as cost-effective networks many times before the 2015 Order went into effect, the federal government's inconsistency and uncertainty about the Internet has dramatic ramifications at the state and local levels. When the FCC and federal courts clash over the

Internet's status, under-served cities are the losers of those battles. More than 20 states have laws restricting municipal broadband, and without federal intervention, private companies will continue to hold cities, counties, and townships at their mercy.

Municipal broadband projects are, therefore, a nexus of administrative challenges ranging from federal politics all the way down to local cost-benefit analyses. Given this complexity, it is small wonder they have not become ubiquitous in the United States. But these challenges are not insurmountable, and the following analysis will prove it.

Local governments can and should solve their own Internet access problems to drive local economic development, invigorate their communities, and take control of their own future. This analysis offers the understanding and guidance they need to get started.

II. THE POLITICS OF MUNICIPAL BROADBAND.

1. Municipal Broadband Is Not a Partisan Issue.

FCC leadership's sharply split votes along party lines do not mean a party split is a sure thing at all levels of government. At the state, county, and city levels, municipal broadband has advocates in both parties. The political conflicts in municipal broadband are not party versus party, but public versus private.

In Tennessee, for example, state senator Janice Bowling (R) introduced legislation in 2017 to end a restriction affecting numerous municipal broadband projects. Municipal broadband often comes from an existing electrical utility provider that leverages its infrastructure to build out Internet service. Tennessee law currently restricts the broadband service area from a municipal electric utility to the area covered by the electric service. This restriction means larger municipalities with the capability to reach their neighbors in underserved communities are prevented from doing so (Gonzalez, 2017).

Bowling's republican affiliation matters less than her hometown of Tullahoma, one of the cities affected by current restrictions. As with much of the wave of new legislation about municipal broadband, Bolling's bill (SB 1058) and its companion bill in the House (HB 0970) remain undecided.

<table><tr><td>

Policy at Your Fingertips:
SB 1058:
http://www.capitol.tn.gov/Bills/110/Bill/SB1058.pdf
HB 0970:
http://www.capitol.tn.gov/Bills/110/Bill/HB0970.pdf

</td></tr></table>

In North Carolina, state representatives cooperated across party lines to introduce legislation to allow the city of Wilson to include its entire county and the neighboring municipality of Pinetops. The representatives, Susan Martin (R) and Jean Farmer-Butterfield (D), both come from Wilson, which provides a high-capacity fiber-optic service called Greenlight. This fiber-to-the-home (FTTH) network included Pinetops. But when "the U.S. Court of Appeals for the 9th Circuit reversed the FCC's preemption of state law restricting [the] geographical reach of broadband from municipal electric utilities," North Carolina's existing laws meant Wilson could no longer sell broadband outside of its borders—including to Pinetops (Gonzalez, 2017).

HB 396 was passed in June 2017, allowing Greenlight to serve Pinetops at least until another provider chooses to serve the city. The law affirms community well-being matters more than partisan disputes. It also shows the policy problem caused by the United States Court of Appeals for the Sixth Circuit's 2016 decision to rebuff the FCC's preemption of state laws on municipal broadband. See the section on Chattanooga for details on this decision.

Municipalities can no longer rely on the FCC to

push aside legal barriers at the state level. Instead, the push to establish municipal broadband in North Carolina and similar states must come from within the state. The battle does not pit party against party, but cities and counties against the restrictive laws lobbied for and often written by private companies.

Policy at Your Fingertips:
HB 396:
http://www.ncleg.net/Sessions/2017/Bills/House/PD
F/H396v0.pdf

2. What Are the Restrictions, and Who Benefits?

The beneficiaries are cable companies and private internet service providers. Their lobbies pressure state legislatures. Lobby pressure from Verizon, for example, contributed to the passage of state law in Philadelphia which explicitly prohibits municipal broadband (Dunne, p. 1127, 1136–7). These lobbies even write the legislation, and this is no secret.

For example, SB 304 in Kansas was written by the Kansas Cable Telecommunications Association (KCTA), a fact reported in such popular news sources as Fox News (Stewart, 2014). The 2014 bill's full name was the Municipal Communications Network and Private Telecommunications Investment Safeguards Act, and its real intent was to "safeguard" the cable industry. It would have prevented Kansas municipalities from "offer[ing] or provid[ing] to one or more subscribers, video, telecommunications, or broadband service." This bill was eventually defeated

(Teters, 2015, p. 93).

Cable lobbies have good friends in state legislatures—the best friends money can buy. "According to the Kansas Ethics Commission, the Cable Television lobby spent more than $43,000 in 2013 wining and dining state lawmakers, with AT&T spending $25,003.86. [KCTA President John] Federico spent $8,383.92 lobbying on behalf of the cable television industry" (Stewart, 2014).

While the Kansas bill would have prevented cities from offering communications services to any areas except the completely unserved, other statutes seek to restrict the area by political boundary. North Carolina's HB 129 typifies this in a requirement in §160A-340.1(3): city-owned communications service providers must "limit the provision of communications service to within the corporate limits of the city providing the communications service."

These are not isolated incidents but a widespread phenomenon affecting more than 20 states. Missouri's SB 186, introduced in early 2017, and North Carolina's HB 129, which passed in 2011, are but two examples of restrictive legislation pushed by cable companies. The trend continues right up to the present, with no end in sight.

In October 2017, Michigan's state legislature saw HB 5099 introduced and sent to committee, and the bill "would ban Michigan towns and cities from using taxpayer funds to build or operate community broadband networks" (Bode, 2017). Michigan Representative Michele Hoitenga introduced the bill, and it should come as no surprise that her largest campaign contributors included AT&T Michigan, the Telecommunications Association of Michigan, and the Michigan Cable Telecommunications Association. The bill makes little sense when we consider, as we will see in the section of Financing, that taxes are rarely if ever needed to fund a municipal network.

Policy at Your Fingertips:
SB 186: http://www.senate.mo.gov/17info/pdf-bill/intro/SB186.pdf
HB 129:
http://www.ncga.state.nc.us/Sessions/2011/Bills/House/PDF/H129v3.pdf
HB 5099:
https://www.legislature.mi.gov/documents/2017-2018/billintroduced/House/pdf/2017-HIB-5099.pdf

---

GUIDES TO STATE RESTRICTIONS

As these restrictions vary from state to state, creating an exhaustive list is problematic. New bills are introduced every year, so any list risks becoming quickly obsolete in the dynamic world of public policy. But, attempts have been made.

Attorney James Baller of the Baller Herbst Law Group compiled a list in 2014:
https://ecfsapi.fcc.gov/file/7521826169.pdf

In January 2015, FCC Commissioner Michael O'Rielly published a chart summarizing state-by-state restrictions:
https://www.fcc.gov/news-events/blog/2015/01/30/municipal-broadband-snapshot

In his summary of state-level restrictions, Commissioner O'Rielly questioned the FCC's authority to pre-empt state laws, but he also pointed out that not every restriction is unreasonable. Public hearings and formal cost-benefit analyses are statutory requirements he sees as reasonable and achievable.

But regarding prohibitions against localities offering "telecommunications service as defined by federal law" in Nevada, O'Reilly's chart exemplifies the constant shifts in policy on this topic. He wrote, "Broadband is not treated currently as a telecommunications service by the FCC, so this isn't a limitation" (O'Rielly, 2015). But a month later, the 2015 Open Internet Order changed that, so any restriction on "telecommunications services" certainly covers broadband. Should the new FCC administration under Chairman Pai overturn this aspect of the 2015 Order, this might be the one silver lining, since presumably Nevada cities could then offer Internet service.

Either way, the political climate in many states is hostile to municipal broadband projects and friendly to the interests of private cable companies and ISPs.

3. Municipal Broadband in Arizona.

The Institute for Local Self-Reliance, a municipal broadband advocacy group, does not consider Arizona a state with restrictive legislation[1]. The state's political climate is more hospitable than many to municipal networks. Arizona Senator John McCain (R), along with Frank Lutenberg (D-NJ), co-sponsored the Community Broadband Act of 2005 (S.1294) at the federal level to "protect local government authority to offer advanced communications services" (Dingwall, 2006, p. 87). The bill would have amended the Telecommunications Act of 1996 to eliminate all state and local government prohibitions against public telecommunications:

> "No State or local government statute, regulation, or other State or local government legal requirement may prohibit, or have the effect of prohibiting, any public provider from providing advanced telecommunications capability, or services using advanced telecommunications capability, to any person or any public or private entity."

In its third section, the bill would have required public providers to give private companies an opportunity to bid on providing the desired services, a clear yet reasonable concession to cable company arguments about competition. But Congress never passed this act. When it was reintroduced as S.1853, the Community Broadband Act of 2007, it also died in Congress. Federal legislators are not yet ready to give the entire nation the freedom Arizona's municipalities have to serve their own citizens with broadband access.

Policy at Your Fingertips:
HB 129:
http://www.ncga.state.nc.us/Sessions/2011/Bills/Ho use/PDF/H129v7.pdf
S.1853:
https://www.govtrack.us/congress/bills/110/s1853/te xt

Due to its unrestrictive environment, Arizona has given rise to several municipal broadband projects, and most have enjoyed varying degrees of success. One, a less-than-successful wireless mesh network in Tempe, will be explored in the section on Fail Factors.

Another, the Tohono O'odham Utility Authority currently provides DSL service to a limited area. This was made possible as part of a $33.6 million federal stimulus package of grants and loans affecting four Native American reservations (Hansen, 2011). $17.4 million went directly to the Tohono O'odham Utility Authority to build 150 miles of fiber optic cable and install wireless towers in underserved areas (ibid).

The City of Mesa has been building and expanding its fiber optic infrastructure for more than a decade, encouraging its use by independent providers and areas in need of economic development, and bringing to the city new business operations such as the Apple Global Command Center (Community, 2015). When city streets are excavated for construction, Mesa uses the opportunity to build onto its fiber network which now has more than 150 miles of fiber (Gonzalez, 2015).

Mesa's electricity is provided by a publicly owned utility, which makes it somewhat unique in Arizona, where most electricity is provided by 15 private corporations (ACC, 2017, p. 1). These companies are governed by the Arizona Corporation Commission (ACC). But the ACC does not oversee public, municipal utilities.

Like Mesa, the Salt River Project (SRP) also provides Internet service in Arizona, including fiber-optic connections available to approximately 13,000 people (BroadbandNow, 2017). SRP provides electric service as a municipal utility not overseen by the ACC, because it originally began as a public irrigation project and has maintained that status in the ACC's eyes (ACC, 2017). Mesa and SRP are important to consider because they are examples of a theme explored in more depth in the Success Factors section: existing public utility infrastructures are an excellent starting point for building fiber optic networks in municipal broadband projects.

Public electricity companies are not the only utilities serving Arizona with fiber-optic connections. A few Arizona communities near the Utah border receive connectivity from South Central Communications (SCC), a cooperative which began in 1953 as the South Central Utah Telephone

Association (Gonzalez, 2016).

Arizona is home to several organizations promoting the growth of municipal broadband, including the Arizona Rural Development Council, Local First Arizona Foundation, and Gila River Telecommunications. The latter is owned and operated by the Gila River Indian Community and provides low-cost Internet service to the area's homes and businesses (Gila, 2017).

And, in April 2017, Mesa hosted the Digital Southwest Regional Broadband Summit, featuring keynote speaker Mignon Clyburn, an FCC Commissioner who briefly served as the FCC's Acting Chairwoman in 2013 (FCC, 2017). (She also voted against repealing net neutrality provisions in the FCC's December 2017 vote.) This conference brought together public and private providers to discuss the future of municipal broadband in Arizona. That future looks bright, and Arizona's lack of restrictive state laws exemplifies the political and legal environment so many states currently lack. Where they are not hampered by restrictive cable company legislation, municipal networks thrive.

4. The FCC's Role.

Municipalities in restrictive states have petitioned the Federal Communications Commission (FCC) to step in and allow them to create broadband networks and serve areas beyond their existing utility's service area. Pre-emption means the federal agency overrides existing state laws. The FCC's authority to pre-empt state laws was called into question in court and ultimately denied at the Circuit Court level in 2016 (Howard, 2017, p. 14–15).

Since the turn of the century, many writings have analyzed and attempted to form a legal justification for the FCC's authority to pre-empt these laws. Most often, the arguments hinge on language in the Telecommunications Act of 1996 which appears to give the FCC authority to take actions to promote competition and remove barriers to entry in telecommunications markets. The reasoning in these arguments has become less relevant since the enactment of the FCC's 2015 Open Internet Order, as most who favored pre-emption focused on how the FCC did not consider broadband a *telecommunications* service but an *information* service. The 2015 order changed that (summarizing Howard, 2015).

In the *Columbia Law Review*, Matthew Dunne examined the legal foundation for the power of pre-emption by a federal administrative agency, and concluded from case law that agencies can pre-empt if they have been explicitly granted that power by federal legislation (Dunne, 2007, p. 1140–2). The question becomes one of interpreting the vague 1996 Act, which is the legislative source of the FCC's authority. Dunne detailed Supreme Court and DC Circuit Court rulings that showed a variety of interpretations of the Act's meaning for the FCC. But because his analysis (and all its cases) predated the 2015 Order, Dunne focused on the old Title I classification of Internet, and the problem of Title II authority was, at the time, completely untested in the courts.

I covered this point and its far-reaching ramifications in detail in *Net Neutrality for Broadband: Understanding the FCC's 2015 Open Internet Order*. With the 2015 Order, broadband became reclassified as a telecommunications service, and it would make sense that the FCC could then pre-empt state laws to enable the expansion of municipal broadband.

For a time, cities petitioned the FCC to do just that. The FCC was pre-empting state laws in 2015, such as Kansas legislation that affected the city of Chanute, which will be explored in this paper in greater detail. The FCC found its legal foundation for overriding state laws in §706 of the 1996 Act, which "directs the FCC to 'encourage the deployment on a reasonable and timely basis of advanced telecommunications capability to all Americans' through "measures that promote competition in the local telecommunications market, or other regulating methods that remove barriers to infrastructure investment" (Teters, 2015, p. 107–8).

But the FCC was blocked by a ruling from United States Court of Appeals for the Sixth Circuit, as discussed in the section on Chattanooga. Not everyone at the FCC was upset about it. FCC leadership's stance on pre-emption was based on a mixed vote. At the time, Chairman Ajit Pai was a Commissioner, and he voted against it. Former Chairman Wheeler, who supported pre-emption, is now gone, and even supporters of pre-emption must admit its legal basis was shaky to begin with. This court's ruling, combined with the FCC's alterations to net neutrality regulation in December 2017, makes one thing clear: if municipalities want to take control of their Internet and economic futures, they will need to do it without the FCC's intervention.

5. Competition and Public Utilities: A Philosophy for Broadband Policy.

"There is a growing recognition that the corporate, proprietary models do not allow the kind of innovation necessary; and that the communications infrastructure must be reclaimed as a public utility" (Kidd, p. 19).

Cable company and private ISP claims that municipal broadband threatens them are hard to swallow. Take as one example Verizon, who backed the legislation prohibiting municipal broadband in Pennsylvania. With more than $244 billion in assets, and $130 billion in revenue generating $17 billion in profit in 2016, Verizon ranks as the thirtieth largest corporation in the world, including state-owned enterprises (DeCarlo, 2016). It's difficult to see how America's cities pose any real threat to Verizon's existence.

Nevertheless, private ISPs, their lobbies, and their lawyers continue to put forth arguments about the threat municipalities pose, and the necessity of policy measures to contain that threat. This rhetoric follows by-now predictable lines and is exemplified by a 2006 article by attorney Craig Dingwall in the *Federal Communications Law Journal.* At the time, he represented "telecommunications, cable, and information technology providers before federal and state regulators" (Dingwall, 2006, p. 67).

Dingwall argued the federal government needs to step in to "level the playing field" so private companies can remain competitive with municipalities. He argued municipalities should be *compelled* to accept bids from private companies prior to building their own, which they should only do if they receive no bids or if there is no existing service in their market (ibid, p. 101). Dingwall's other policy suggestions make it clear he wanted broadband to expand, but only under a policy regime restricting municipalities from innovating their own solutions. He advocated maintaining market opportunities for private ISPs, and believed they could adequately serve municipalities.

But the truth is, and the ten years since his essay have borne this out, that private ISPs lack incentive to reach many communities; and even if they wanted to, the need for high-speed connections has grown faster than private companies can supply it.

The primary argument advanced by cable companies and private ISPs is this: municipalities have existing infrastructure they can leverage to build their own broadband networks, giving them an unfair competitive advantage over private companies. The idea of competition, however, is being misused when the situation involves a public entity.

Public entities, after all, are nothing more than the people acting collectively through institutions. When public entities create their own infrastructure, they are people collectively acting to meet their own needs. From providing utilities to resurfacing city streets, municipalities enjoy the same freedom individuals do to meet their own needs in a way of their own choosing.

Blocking a municipality from meeting the public's needs on its own, without using a privately owned network, is the equivalent of telling a person he cannot mow his own lawn, or wash his own clothes, or cook his own food. People can meet their own needs through their own efforts, and should not be restricted from this freedom simply because a private company is being shut out from providing the service. Cooking one's own dinner with one's own equipment eliminates the need for relying on privately owned restaurants, but no one would suggest barring citizens from preparing food so that private companies can profit from the same enterprise.

In the same way, a city or county that creates its own broadband service does not need a privately owned ISP. But this has nothing to do with anti-competitive business practices and an American regulatory tradition of restraining private monopolies. The government may regulate private business to preserve competition, but public entities represent people, not private corporations. As such, public entities should not be considered part of the competition argument.

This perspective on competition is far from radical. Former Chairman of the Federal Trade Commission (FTC) Jon Leibowitz made similar arguments in his presentation at the 25th annual conference of the National Association of Telecommunications Officers and Advisors. In a speech entitled "Municipal Broadband: Should Cities Have a Voice", he said:

> "To put this in context, imagine if Borders and Barnes & Noble, claiming it was killing their book sales, asked lawmakers to ban cities from building libraries. The legislators would laugh them out of the State House. Yet the same thing is happening right now with respect to Wi-Fi and other municipal broadband plans, and it is being taken all too seriously" (Leibowitz, 2005, p. 1).

If municipalities can provide broadband for their constituents in fiscally responsible, technologically advanced ways which provide greater coverage and generate revenue for public funds, then they have every right to do so, regardless of legislative trends to the contrary in many states.

Politicians and their appointees who favor private business as the solution for all American ills oppose public broadband networks. From state legislatures to the upper echelon of the FCC, many policy makers would prefer to see the public cut out of the broadband business.

This explains many objections to the 2015 Open Internet Order, for its core is the reclassification of broadband under Title II as a common-carrier service, or, put in layman's terms, a public utility. The genius of the Order is its recognition that people now require fast, reliable Internet connections with the same urgency they require other utilities to survive in modern society, and to maintain an adequate standard of living.

Like clean, running water and dependable electricity, telecommunications have become a necessity, not a luxury, if people want things we all agree are parts of a modern standard of living: access to high-quality education to advance one's station in life, access to employment opportunities to earn a living, access to health care services, connection to a community, and involvement in political processes such as voting. Broadband Internet access "is seen by many governments as a public utility, similar to that of water, gas, electricity, and waste, rather than a luxury" (Tapia, 2010, p. 94).

Could humans survive without Internet? Obviously. They can also survive without electric power and bath water, without housing, without hospitals, and without civil rights. But that is hardly what we would consider participating in modern society, and the person without a bed, alarm clock, and shower stall will have a tough time winning that next job interview—if they ever get a chance to set one up.

But policy makers who favor private enterprise would have voters believe that Internet is a luxury item, and that market forces will provide adequate distribution of this luxury to those who demand it. Nothing could be farther from the truth for municipalities across the country who remain underserved by the same corporations lobbying to prevent those municipalities from solving their own problem.

Thus, the potential erosion of the 2015 Open Internet Order has far greater implications for the public than the headline-grabbing "net neutrality" rules against throttling, blocking, and paid prioritization. The Order's reclassification of broadband as a utility provides a policy foundation for public entities to provide that utility to their people. Tearing down that foundation would put more than just fast downloads at risk. It would "cripple a local government's ability to address the economic and social needs of its community, and submit the municipality to the will of the ISP" (Teters, 2015, p. 109).

This is not to say private business has no place in broadband, even publicly owned networks. Many successful municipal projects have engaged the private sector to build and manage publicly owned projects, and the financial success of many public networks owes, in part, to leasing their capacity to private companies who use and resell the services. But in these cases, the municipality retains control, and the profits generated for the private companies in these partnerships come with corresponding profits for the public entity. Such is the proper role for private business in the new era of broadband as a utility, regardless of how little the cable companies desire giving up control to the people.

A municipality does have an advantage over

telecoms and ISPs if it already has a public utility infrastructure—typically electricity—which gives it "free access to public assets that can be used to mount network infrastructure equipment" (King, 2014, p. 76). This contributes to the argument that municipalities have an unfair competitive advantage over private companies—a point rendered moot when private companies have left a community underserved. In the words of former FCC Commissioner Michael Copps, municipal broadband should be "encouraged", not "hobbled" by bills that say, "You can't do this because it's interfering with somebody's idea of the functioning marketplace," because "the marketplace is not functioning in those places" (Hu, 2005).

The cry of "unfair advantage" makes little sense. It is more unfair to tell a city it cannot use its own existing infrastructure to solve the problem of delivering a public good such as Internet service, and must instead wait for sub-standard service at greater costs from a private corporation with little intention of serving the community.

III. SUCCESS FACTORS: POSITIVE RESULTS FROM MUNICIPAL BROADBAND.

This section explores successful municipal broadband projects and draws definite conclusions from those successes. Readers unfamiliar with the abbreviations for the various types of fiber networks should consult the Appendix for clarification.

These examples were chosen based on their availability in peer-reviewed literature and writings by administrators involved in the networks' creation and management, but they are by no means unique. The success they enjoyed is widespread in similar projects across the country. This analysis reveals the roots of those successes.

1. Lake County, FL: Planning for Economic Growth.

A 2005 study of a municipal fiber optic project in Lake County, Florida, found strong empirical evidence that the project led to stronger economic growth in the county compared to eight similar counties lacking such a project. By comparing "county-level data on gross sales" in the years before and after the project's implementation, researchers found Lake County's growth rate was more than double that of the control group (Ford, 2005, p. 221).

Researchers noted that Lake County "experienced relatively rapid population growth" during the years studied, so they repeated their analysis a second time, on a per-capita basis. Again, they found an economic growth rate more than double the control group's (ibid, p. 225–226).

The researchers recognized that Lake County's population growth, which is also used as an indicator of economic development in some models, could have a direct relationship with the fiber-optic initiative (ibid, p. 225). After all, as the service becomes available, the community attracts and retains citizens and businesses who value the service.

Another important aspect of the Florida study is the observation that privately owned broadband networks in comparable counties "did not produce the sizeable growth" observed in Lake County. Researchers pointed to the difference in the way municipally owned broadband captures for the city or county many benefits that go beyond a private company's bottom line (ibid, p. 227). In other words, a private company making a profit by selling its service or leasing its private infrastructure does not capture other economic benefits that pervade the community. If a city or county attracts businesses and residents, they participate in the overall economic development of the community, from housing developments and sales taxes to a more vibrant labor pool, all from a system that can generate income for the city.

The overall benefits to a municipality, captured holistically at the municipal level, offer strong encouragement to deploy infrastructure that serves the entire community by reaching every home and business. Private companies lack this incentive, and are more strongly incentivized to focus their service and infrastructure development on areas with high population densities and high incomes. This leads to one of the most common arguments in favor of municipal broadband: private companies are underserving many communities due to a lack of profit incentives, but municipalities can reap major economic benefits from serving those very same communities.

Thinking of broadband networks as part of a "community's public infrastructure" puts them alongside roads, schools, transportation, access to health care, and other "quality of life" factors that "attract new businesses and residents" (ibid, p. 216). It also reverses the flow of revenue. Rather than the public entity paying private networks for connectivity, the public entity generates income by offering connectivity to private businesses and by leasing its infrastructure and bandwidth to private companies. The Lake County project began when the City of Leesburg, in 2001, "began offering private businesses across Lake County access to one of Florida's most extensive, municipally owned broadband networks, with fiber-optic connections to hospitals, doctor offices, private businesses, and 44 schools" (ibid, p. 218).

Success Factors:
- The city developed a solid plan to generate revenue and obtain paying customers.
- The city began with existing public utility infrastructure.

- The city chose a fiber-optic system that provides high speed and high capacity to meet future demand, and which lays a foundation for expansion.

2. Danville, VA: Strategizing for an Economic Turnaround.

By the turn of the century, Danville had experienced 20 years of economic and population decline as its legacy industries of tobacco and textiles withered away (King, 2014, p. 36). With a goal of shifting "its traditional manufacturing and agricultural economy to a more diversified knowledge-based economy capable of creating and sustaining family-wage jobs", and faced with the harsh reality of losing "a recruitment competition for a large data center," Danville launched nDanville to transform the city. Instead of waiting for private companies to build infrastructure in its isolated rural area, Danville leveraged its own infrastructure.

Though the city had economic problems, it was a "municipal electricity distributor serving a 500-square-mile territory," which meant Danville "had the opportunity to make use of its power poles and utility rights-of-way to deploy fiber cable", and also "workforce resources" and "equipment" to support the project (ibid, p. 37). This decision points to two success factors in municipal broadband projects. One, a municipality with experience and infrastructure providing other public utilities (such as electricity) has a strong foundation for providing broadband as a utility. Two, Danville made sure it had a good reason for picking its particular technology.

By analyzing the needs of the businesses it hoped to attract, Danville realized its technology needed to provide both *very* high-speed Internet *and* "direct point-to-point connectivity between multiple business locations" (ibid, p. 38). Only a network based on running fiber to the premises (FTTP) would meet that need. Danville combined that network with a Wi-Fi service to provide coverage in public areas such as city parks, where the fiber ends at antennae in the parks.

Danville's success owes to a third factor: a thorough analysis of its business model, an analysis which determined that competing with private companies for TV-based entertainment would be too expensive and potentially disastrous (ibid, p. 39). Danville settled on an "open access business model" where nDanville directly provides service to public entities such as schools and libraries, and then allows private companies to operate on the network to provide service to businesses and residences. The private companies share revenue from these operations with the city, and the high-speed connectivity has attracted international businesses to the community.

As nDanville continues to expand through second and third phases of implementation which increase its coverage, services, and quality to more and more customers, City Manager Joe King believes the network has grown more slowly than other business models might have allowed. But in this case, careful attention to its choice of business model has made nDanville a financially stable and profitable enterprise. It is debt-free, as the expansions are paid for as they happen and have been fully funded by user fees. "Without taxpayer or utility ratepayer subsidies," nDanville "contributes $300,000 annually to the City's General Fund" with a total investment to mid-2014 of $15 million.

Success Factors:
- The city adequately assessed the community's needs for service, and clearly defined the local government's role in meeting those needs.
- The city selected a suitable business model and financial plan, then carefully developed a strategy to implement the system.
- The city used existing public utility infrastructure as the foundation for building the network.

3. Chanute, KS: Fiber for the Future, and Federal Involvement.

Chanute tackled the problem of broadband expansion without relying on private cable companies or the FCC's subsidies. Instead of waiting for expensive last-mile infrastructure to come to it, Chanute built its own (Lefler, 2014). Yet despite the success of its network and the resultant economic growth it spurred, Chanute faced litigation from private ISPs who argued the municipal project was illegal. It also confronted a bill in the state legislature "that would have outlawed community broadband systems in Kansas"—a bill written by "a cable TV industry group" (ibid).

Chanute's fiber optic network has its origins in 1984, when the City Utility Department "built a fiber-optic network to improve electricity network management" (Teters, 2015, p. 106). But this limited-use network was insufficient to bring high-speed Internet to the entire municipality. Chanute expanded this fiber-optic network to bring one-gigabit speeds to residents, schools, emergency responders, and businesses, and it constructed a wireless network, too (ibid). Chanute's expansion, which began in 2005, now includes a project to expand even further to create a fiber-to-the-home (FTTH) network at a proposed cost of $13.5 million, and bring one-gigabit speeds to the community (Lefler, 2014).

Expanding the electric utility's infrastructure was part of Chanute's success, but so was smart money management. City officials estimated the network would pay for itself within ten years (ibid).

Success Factors:
- The municipality created a sustainable financial plan so the network could generate revenue and pay for itself in a reasonable time.
- The robust fiber-optic network delivers high speeds, provides a backbone for future expansion, and lays a solid foundation for the future.

- The city leveraged existing electrical utility infrastructure.

4. Chattanooga, TN: Synergy between Electric Utilities and Internet.

Chattanooga's insufficient Internet capabilities resembled those of other cities in this analysis: private ISPs had not invested in developing the city's broadband infrastructure, and had "no immediate plans" to do so (Teters, 2015, p. 95). Building on two decades of improving its economy and environment, Chattanooga received in 2009 a $111 million stimulus grant from the federal government and built its own solution (Wyatt, 2014).

Now nicknamed "Gig City", Chattanooga boasts a fiber-optic, gigabit-per-second Internet service which has drawn new business to the city and "$4 billion in foreign investment" (Teters, 2015, p. 96). Quickcue exemplifies the development and innovation the new gigabit speeds brought to the city. As a startup in 2011, creating a "tablet-based guest-management system for restaurants", Quickcue drew $3 million in investments and was sold in 2013 for $11.5 million (Wyatt, 2014). Residents also enjoy a less expensive option of 100 megabits per second, "which is still faster than many other places in the country" (ibid).

Chattanooga's power company, Electric Power Board (EPB), played the key role in this economic and technologic development. The company had a need for improved Internet to create more efficient monitoring and management of its power grid, and it had an existing infrastructure connected to homes and businesses (Teters, 2015, p. 95). EPB became more than a power company; it became a public ISP, too. This capacity to leverage existing utility infrastructure to create high-speed Internet is a hallmark of successful municipal broadband projects, one appearing in case study after case study.

EPB also tiered its pricing and services so users could obtain slower yet still robust speeds at a lower monthly cost (Wyatt, 2014). This flexibility in meeting consumer demand is one of Chattanooga's success factors. It allows for more widespread adoption of the service for residents of all income levels.

But not every public Internet initiative is successful, and Chattanooga experienced a failure that echoes that of Tempe, Arizona. Like Tempe, Chattanooga spent "millions" to develop a wireless mesh network that went "largely unused" by residents and public agencies (ibid).

Chattanooga also fought an uphill battle against state laws restricting it from expanding its service areas beyond the municipality's borders. As I wrote in *Two Years with Net Neutrality*:

"EPB, the municipal utility serving Chattanooga, TN, petitioned the FCC to allow it to deliver Internet to communities outside of the 600-square mile area they service (Settles, 2014). Wilson, NC petitioned to provide Internet to local communities, and the FCC determined residents who lived outside the service range of utility companies in Chattanooga and Wilson had no broadband service at all (Gross, 2015).

"The states challenged the FCC's interference, and the legal authority behind it. In August 2016, 'the United States Court of Appeals for the Sixth Circuit upheld restrictive laws in North Carolina and Tennessee that will halt the growth of such networks' (Kang, 2016). While the court agreed that municipal networks were valuable, it disagreed with the FCC's legal arguments on its power to pre-empt state laws (ibid). The court ruled the FCC could not block North Carolina and Tennessee 'from setting limits on municipal broadband expansion' (Reuters, 2016)" (Howard, 2017, p. 14–15).

As with several other examples in this paper, such as Philadelphia and Pinetops, Chattanooga's EPB found it needed bipartisan support in the state legislature to overcome the laws. The Circuit Court of Appeals' decision has established that municipalities will no longer be able to rely on the FCC to step in and "fix" their state-level problems.

Success Factors:
- Broadband was built out from existing public electric utility infrastructure.
- The fiber-optic network provided speeds which were superior to those of private competitors.
- Improved Internet was part of a greater plan for city-wide economic development.

- Federal stimulus funds helped made the development possible.
- The fiber-optic network offers a robust capacity that can handle future increases in broadband demand.
- The utility offered flexibility in pricing tiers and service speeds to meet users' needs.
- Tennessee enjoys bipartisan support for communities who wish to meet their own broadband needs, so Chattanooga could carve its own path without the FCC's pre-emptive assistance.

5. Bristol, VA: Politics and Organizational Flexibility.

Bristol, VA faced legal barriers, private ISP opposition, and financial challenges. BVU, the utility company in Bristol, needed to have a state law overturned before it could manage its own fiber-optic, gigabit network. Then, when Sprint tried to block BVU on the grounds that Sprint's rates were being undercut, federal regulators stepped in (Teters, 2015, p. 100).

"Although the Commission denied Sprint's petition, it did find that BVU's internal rate of return on equity" suggested it was not "earning its cost of capital on the jointly provided telephone, data, and cable services offered via OptiNet," and that there was a "possibility that Bristol's telephone services may be subsidized" (Dingwall, 2006, p. 92–3, quoting the FCC's final order in *Petition of United Telephone-*

Southeast, Inc. for Declaratory Judgment).

But BVU's financial future was not so grim as Dingwall predicted in 2006. In 2009, BVU was "severed from the municipality and turned into an independent authority in the state's possession", a move which created an opportunity for BVU "to continue its expansion efforts to hopefully cover all of southwestern Virginia" (Teters, 2015, p. 101). By 2012, BVU had rolled out gigabit Internet speeds, and its subscriber base reached nearly 12,000 (ibid).

While BVU remained, in this capacity, heavily regulated to prevent undue competition in Virginia, this development at the state level suggests that even in states where municipal broadband faces stern opposition from private corporations and legislatures, municipally based projects may have a future as state-level projects. What began as a municipal project for BVU grew into a service with the potential to cover a service area far beyond its geographical and original service boundaries.

Success Factors:
- The municipality fought to overturn restrictive state laws.
- The FCC played an active role in denying a private ISP's attempt to block the project.
- The municipal utility reorganized as a state-controlled utility to meet local regulatory requirements and still serve the public beyond its original service area.

IV. FAIL FACTORS: EVALUATING TERMINATED PROJECTS.

This section evaluates several projects that failed, but it would more accurate to call most of them disappointments rather than total failures. In many cases, ownership of the networks reverted to the municipality from the hands of private companies hired to build them, and the networks continue to provide cost reductions to the local governments which use them. Their status as failures owes to their inability to fully realize the intended results and stated policy goals.

Several instructive themes emerge from this analysis. First, cities shoot themselves in the foot when they completely entrust private companies with the responsibility of developing, building, managing, and monetizing these networks. Second, handing out free Internet access and expecting that alone to solve a myriad of social ills is a recipe for disappointment. Third, a wireless network might have a lower initial cost to build when compared to fiber optics, but its advantages are correspondingly lower. Fourth, attempts to monetize a local wireless network, especially when access is given out for free, often meet with failure.

Tempe, AZ is given lengthy consideration here, and not only due to its being in the author's home state. Tempe's experiment reinforces lessons from other locales, and its well-documented but lackluster results correspond with disappointments revealed in literature on other cities. Where other technologies failed, such as in LaGrange, GA, the doomed philosophy underpinning Tempe's policy goals finds its echo.

This section draws definite conclusions from these failures and answers the question of why some municipal broadband projects fail and, in fact, were destined to fail from the very beginning.

1. St. Cloud, FL: Budget Challenges and Inadequate Communication.

St. Cloud's wireless expansion project demonstrates how some networks which did not meet their goals still provide benefits and cost savings to a city. While some might judge the network a failure, it could also be called a partial success.

St Cloud had a limited wireless service and sought in 2006 to expand it to cover the entire city. Though many in the community wanted to keep the new network, some residents did not "fully understand" its purpose, and "some customers" expected "far more than was feasible from the network" (Teters, 2015, p. 103).

Though the network was closed for general use in 2009 due to budget constraints, it remained viable for the city's government and public agencies (ibid). 2009 estimates projected the network would reduce the city's costs by $600,000 annually (Vos, 2009). This shows how even a failure to completely realize a project's stated goals can result in a network which financially benefits a municipality.

Fail Factors:
- Inadequate budgeting.
- Inadequate communication to users about the network's capabilities and purpose.

2. Philadelphia, PA: Partial Success and Partial Failure.

Like St. Cloud, Philadelphia eventually closed its municipal network to general use in 2013, but retained it for "emergency services and cost savings" (Teters, 2015, p. 103).

Philadelphia's municipal project traveled a rocky road filled with obstacles and pitfalls, all of which are instructive to future projects. To begin with, Pennsylvania had passed legislation completely prohibiting municipal broadband, but "Philadelphia was effectively grandfathered in" (Dunne, 2007, p. 1127). While planning for its 2004 Wireless Philadelphia project, "the city faced opposition from large ISPs Verizon and Comcast, as well as legislative trouble from the state" (Teters, 2015, p. 102).

The planning committee recommended forming a public-private partnership to run Wireless Philadelphia, but the city's leaders instead went with a "small, private company" to develop, maintain, and own the network (ibid). This decision proved crippling when "the private company was incapable of delivering on its promises" (ibid, p. 103).

This company was Earthlink, which originally contracted in 2005 build the network, and then pulled out in 2008 (Albanesius, 2009). Eventually, the

Network Acquisition Company (NAC) purchased the network, though Philadelphia exercised an option to buy the system from NAC for $2 million (ibid). The city retained the network for use by the government—far from the goal of serving the entire community, but not a total failure.

Fail Factors:
- The private contractor was given control, then backed out of the deal.

3. Tempe, AZ: Bad Choices in Private Partners, Technology, and Goals.

Like Philadelphia, Tempe contracted with a private company which could not fulfill its promises for a wireless network. But that was not the only problem leading to less spectacular results than originally intended.

In 2006, many had high hopes for Tempe's wireless initiative, and Tempe was hailed as the first city in the nation to offer city-wide public-access Wi-Fi. "The city of Tempe boasts the largest ubiquitous border-to-border high-speed broadband network in North America (40 square miles) that provides Wi-Fi access to residents and the business community as well as to its municipal workforce" (Harris, 2006).

The network was called Wireless Access Zone Tempe, or WAZTempe for short, and it included Arizona State University as one of the public institutions users could access at no or low cost (Bain, 2011, p. 4). Tempe used existing infrastructure as a starting point for its wireless network, such as the city's street light poles where antennae could be installed, and its existing fiber backhaul locations (Harris, 2006). NeoReach, a company owned by MobilePro, was chosen to "deploy and manage" the network (Bain, 2011, p. 4).

A public access network would give users free access for two hours, and then charge an hourly fee after that, with the exception that all city government websites would always be accessible at no cost to the user (Harris, 2006). A second network piggybacking on that one would be available for city service workers and municipal employees, such as police officers who could access email and Internet to file reports from the field, utility workers, and traffic engineers (ibid).

In 2006, Dingwall called it a "good example of productive partnering between local government and industry partners" (Dingwall, 2006, p. 82). MobilePro was lauded for "substantially" completing the "installation of a Wi-Fi mesh network available for subscription at all points within the city's borders" (Dunne, 2007, p. 1137).

But the excitement was short-lived, and WAZTempe did not survive much longer in its original form. Tempe still offers free Wi-Fi service, but the WAZTempe brand is long gone (City of Tempe, 2017). Though the network did not catch on as hoped, the city did not lose any money on the deal. "The City of Tempe did not take on any additional costs to build or maintain any of the infrastructures needed for the network," and received "free access to the municipal network for municipal workers on the job" in exchange for offering up its existing resources to MobilePro (Bain, 2011, p. 4).

While this move protected Tempe from financial losses, it placed the entire monetization burden on MobilePro, which ran into financial trouble and failed to profit from the network. Since Tempe did not pay for anything, MobilePro needed "to rely on subscriptions and advertising", neither of which generated enough revenue to "remain in business" (Vos, 2011).

After changing corporate hands a few times, the network ended up in 2007 in the possession of Gobility, which also "ran into financial difficulty", resulting in Tempe's acquisition of the network based on a contractual clause stating that if Gobility abandoned the system, then "Tempe would own all of the Wi-Fi nodes installed on Tempe's street light poles" (ibid).

By that time, the wireless mesh network had been expanded (under ownership by Kite), by "about 600 nodes to improve coverage", bringing the total nodes to "about 1,000" (Lawson, 2007). But many perceived the network as having a low value, because it consisted of "older wireless mesh equipment that many claim did not deliver adequate performance" due to not having enough "access points per square mile"; plus, when "the network was deployed, there were no iPhones and other smartphones" (Vos, 2011). Developments such as 4G wireless mobile service made Tempe's wireless mesh network somewhat irrelevant.

Additionally, Tempe's story is one of several which teaches that "increasing civic engagement" is a policy goal that makes for poor results from a municipal broadband project. The WAZTempe project had stated goals of improving not only city services but improving civic engagement, which means the general public's participation in local government. The latter goal is a recipe for failure, even when the first goal is relatively easy to achieve.

Andrea Tapia, an Assistant Professor of Information Sciences and Technology at Penn State University, generally supports in her analyses the idea that Internet access is a public utility due to its necessity for participation in modern life. But she warns of the dangers awaiting municipal wireless networks (MWN) which naïvely focus on civic engagement. In a 2010 article for *Social Science Computer Review*, she reviewed four cases of MWNs that failed to increase civic engagement.

Her analysis suggests building an MWN to "solve social problems with technology" will potentially backfire if "the original social problem was a poorly engaged public in local and community affairs" (Tapia, 2010, p. 93-4). Tempe's MWN was based, in part, on this desire to "promote usage of the Tempe.gov website and e-government applications by offering free 'anywhere' access to Tempe.gov" (ibid, p. 94).

The desired engagement never happened, which may not be surprising in a college town with a large transient population lives there for a few years for education, then moves elsewhere for a career. Tempe made free wireless available to the downtown college crowd without ever reaching the general population, especially those who lacked Internet access to begin with (ibid, p. 103).

Municipal broadband is not an instant cure for a lack of civic participation in government. Projects based primarily on goals of increasing civic engagement tend to fail, especially when combined with inadequate funding or inadequate knowledge about both the technology and users' needs.

But even projects that fail to increase civic engagement can be successful in other ways: faster, more reliable service; revenue generation; and attracting employers and investors. The bottom line? There must be a more compelling reason to build a municipal network than getting people involved in local government.

Fail Factors:
- The private contractor's inability to profit was exacerbated by its own financial troubles.
- The chosen wireless technology was not forward-thinking enough, and soon became outdone by other wireless developments.
- The stated goal of increased civic engagement was illusory.

4. LaGrange, GA: Misunderstanding Community Needs and Social Dynamics.

In 2000, the mayor of LaGrange, GA attempted to conquer the digital divide affecting his city where a high percentage of the population was minority and low-income residents. It seemed like a grand idea: partner the city government, a private cable company, and a private ISP to provide free Internet access to the entire city of LaGrange. If low-income residents could not afford the monthly $8.70 for the cable TV service bundled with the free Internet, the city subsidized the cable cost completely. The Internet was made available through the set-top box providing the cable television service (Hsieh, 2011, p. 266).

The Internet TV initiative flopped and was terminated after only three years. The private companies failed to realize the expected profits. The ISP, Worldgate, was in bad financial shape anyway, facing bankruptcy, and needed to pull out of the deal. No replacement ISP was found. The program also ran into trouble with the city council, who resisted the $170,000 annual cost of maintaining the subsidized Internet, despite some benefits to the economically disadvantaged residents (ibid, p. 274).

A study of LaGrange published in *The Information Society* focused on other problems of perception and implementation: more affluent members of the community did not really need the gift of free Internet, and some saw subsidizing it as a waste of time and taxpayer dollars; some of the poor were unable to buy additional PC-related equipment to actually use the service; some viewed the service as slow and inferior; and surveys revealed an undercurrent of racism among affluent groups who believed the people benefitting from the service were also inferior (ibid, p. 275). Yet, surveys revealed the disadvantaged residents who did use the service relied on it heavily or even daily, and found it eased burdens by helping them find information faster and pay bills online (ibid, p. 274).

Hsieh's research team concluded that simply giving free Internet to the poor did not automatically solve their problems, especially as many of them lacked training on using computers and Internet tools. This conclusion is echoed in the *Social Science Computer Review*:

> "...delivering broadband Internet access to citizens does not, in fact, solve problems with civic engagement, public participation, and social exclusion. In other words, merely adding low-cost broadband Internet access to impoverished neighborhoods, without additional educational programs and low-cost devices, may exacerbate these problems. Recent research... suggest[s] that the success of engaging the public projects depends on a variety of factors such as training, education, user perceptions of IT, and the organization's past experience with using IT" (Tapia, 2010, p. 109).

Fail Factors:
- The private ISP partner was financially unstable.
- The unrealistic financial plan resulted in a lack of profits for private partners, and thus became expensive for the city to subsidize.
- No one provided relevant training or

equipment to the intended users, so many could not take advantage of the free Internet access.

- The administration did not evaluate the intended users' needs socially, financially, and technologically.
- The technology of Internet TV was a dubious choice compared to robust, forward-thinking, high-capacity fiber optics.

V. MAKING IT HAPPEN: TECHNOLOGY, FINANCING, AND BUSINESS MODELS.

1. Technology Infrastructure.

There are multiple ways to approach the problem of choosing a technology, from Wi-Fi mesh to fiber-optic cable. With multiple infrastructure options to choose from, it helps to consider technology as just one aspect of a successful project. The technology choice relates to the fundamental goals of service and functionality, because it is the practical part of delivering the service. As technology continues to evolve, a city's solution needs to be flexible enough to adapt and upgrade to the next generation of tech.

Fiber optics are the clear choice for a robust, high-speed, high-capacity technology that withstands the test of time. Fiber provides a backbone for future expansion projects, and the promise of meeting future demands on the network.

Municipal wireless networks have met with limited success or outright failure in many cases, but this results from an overreliance on wireless technology. Wireless makes a good peripheral service when built on a strong backbone of fiber. It brings mobile flexibility so municipal workers in the field can access the primary network. It also enables the municipality to reach underserved areas where fiber has yet to be built.

Wireless networks, which place individual access nodes in a locale, carry a lower implementation cost than fiber, which takes more time and money to build. The expenses of running fiber to every residence or business have prevented, in many cases, private ISPs from investing in this superior technology in areas with lower population density, lower incomes, and greater distance from city centers. From the perspective of private ISPs, it makes sense to keep infrastructure costs low and only engage in readily profitable enterprises.

But those costs are scaled down when dealing with an individual location such as a city or county. While the larger private companies understandably avoid the massive expense of covering the entire nation in fiber, a municipality has only its own area to worry about. The costs are in the millions, not the billions, and the timeline to completion is reduced to a few years rather than decades.

Compared to wireless, fiber is also better positioned to meet future demands, and better positioned for stimulating a city's economic growth. Fiber's gigabit speeds are far more attractive to employers and businesses when considering locations for new offices, and far more competitive when compared to connectivity in other countries.

This is a critical difference between a success story like Danville's and a disappointment like Tempe's. Tempe based its entire initiative on a wireless technology which was soon eclipsed by other improved technologies, but Danville treated wireless like a peripheral add-on to its strong core network of fiber. Cities seeking to attract investors and businesses from around the world to stimulate their local economy would do well to follow Danville's example: build fiber for the future, and supplement it with wireless as needed.

2. Financing.

Some of the projects in this report relied on federal stimulus funds, such as the Tohono O'odham Utility Authority in Arizona. But most municipalities do not need to rely on federal grants and loans to finance their own network. Chattanooga, for example, used internal loans from local governmental departments, as did Spanish Fork, UT and Auburn, IN, to name a few. Issuing revenue bonds to private investors, either through the government or through the utility company building the network, also raises funds, and was used successfully in cities such as Lafayatte, LA, Cedar Falls, IA, and Longmont, CO.[2]

Because municipalities can issue bonds and use interdepartmental loans, they rarely have any need to raise taxes to fund a municipal network. Case studies suggest that taxation is the *least* effective funding choice, because it makes the project unfavorable to both city councils and voters, who may then stall or cancel the project.

Hermosa Beach, CA illustrates how taxes are the wrong way to fund these projects. The city intended to provide free Wi-Fi to its downtown area and fund the monthly cost by selling advertising on the network's initial web page, and the city funded the original construction costs through tax dollars (Park, 2010, p. 436–7). The advertising did not cover the monthly expense, and the project's reliance on taxation made it unfavorable to the city council when expansion was discussed (ibid). The result was a lackluster, under-used Wi-Fi network that failed to grow and failed to recoup investments. This failure also reinforces a lesson from Tempe and other cities: a municipal broadband project needs to be about more than simply installing a wireless network in a downtown area and giving out free access.

Municipalities enjoy far greater financial success when they begin with more aggressive and well-planned broadband initiatives focused on serving a wide customer base which includes the public sector, such as schools, emergency services, utility workers, government facilities, and administrative institutions. When the public sector builds its own network and becomes its own ISP, it reaps tremendous cost reductions that help the project pay for itself in a matter or years and remain financially viable.

These kinds of broadband initiatives cut costs and decrease long-term government spending on Internet access, and the networks provide additional revenue streams for local government: leasing and reselling network access, or selling directly to residential and business customers. Thus, the initial expenses of building or expanding a municipal network are offset by increased income and reduced costs.

While there is no one-size-fits-all cost-benefit analysis that can apply to every possible city, municipalities have repeatedly demonstrated these principles. The Institute for Local Self-Reliance (ILSR) offers many striking examples. In Martin County, FL, the Martin County School District now enjoys a reduction of more than $340,000 every year for a gigabit connection servicing 26 locations, and the city paid off its investment in fiber in 2017. Medina County, OH offers its Highland Public Schools access to the municipal network at an annual reduction of $82,000 compared to what Time Warner Cable charged the schools. In Virginia, Bristol and Martinsville have eliminated millions of dollars in costs for telephone service by building their own networks, and increased their connection speed at the same time.[3]

With more than 400 communities enjoying similar results across the country, an exhaustive list of cost reductions exceeds the scope of this report, but the trend is undeniable. A well-planned municipal network does cost money to build, but it pays for itself over time by driving down the public sector's service costs and generating additional income—and improving service while doing it.

3. Business Models.

Selecting the right business model is a cornerstone of a successful municipal broadband program. Philadelphia and Tempe took a hands-off approach and placed the well-being of their networks entirely in the hands of private companies. But when those companies failed to deliver and backed out of the projects, the cities were left holding the bag. These failures demonstrate the need to thoroughly evaluate the financial condition of any private entity involved. But they also suggest that cities will be better off avoiding these situations altogether by taking a more active and immediate ownership of the networks they need built.

Tempe's struggles after adopting a hands-off approach with a private contractor were echoed in the city of Cerritos, CA. Cerritos used a similar strategy with the private company Aiirmesh deploying a wireless network, and the results were less than satisfactory. Aiirmesh dramatically raised the monthly price of residential service from its initial $29.99 to $49.99, and the downlink speed for that cost was only 768K (Park, 2010, p. 429–432).

Hermosa Beach, CA, encountered similar failures after the private company (LA Unplugged) chosen to build a wireless network for the city went out of business (Park, 2010, p. 436). Management of the network reverted to the city government, but the city government had, as discussed in the Financing section, chosen unsuccessful funding methods, and the project failed to thrive or expand (ibid).

Even so, public-private partnership plays an important role in municipal broadband success stories. Danville's successful business model includes giving private companies access to the municipal network so those companies can sell access to residences and business. This generates profits for both private firms and the municipality which controls the network. This arrangement of leasing network capacity and allowing private companies to resell network access keeps the city in the driver's seat, and creates a more stable and healthy operation for the city than simply giving private companies free rein to do as they please.

4. Summary.

- Build fiber for the future, and supplement it with wireless access as needed.
- Bonds and interdepartmental loans are sufficient to fund most municipal broadband projects without raising taxes. Federal stimulus funds are also available.
- Any analysis of the cost to build the network must also consider subsequent reductions in expenses and the increases in revenue for the municipality.
- Financially successful municipal networks do not simply give away Wi-Fi to downtown areas. They plan to make the public sector its own ISP, thereby reducing costs and improving service.
- Private companies play a role in monetizing a municipal network, but the city needs to retain control of it. Leasing and reselling arrangements are profitable options.
- Conversely, failure awaits projects that give all control to private companies when those contractors abandon the project for financial or other business reasons.

VI. QUICK GUIDE TO SUCCESS AND FAILURE FACTORS.

Social	
Success	**Failure**
• Assess the community's needs for service, and clearly define the local government's role in meeting those needs.	• Ignore the intended users' social realities, financial situations, and technological knowledge; and instead, simply assume the presence of a network will solve social problems.
• Communicate with intended users about the network's capabilities and purposes.	
• Provide training on how people can use the network (and the Internet in general) to meet their needs for social services, ordering goods and services, and educating themselves.	• Do not communicate to users about the network's capabilities and purpose.
	• Assume people can use the technology to solve their own problems without any further guidance or training.
• Offer flexibility in pricing tiers and service speeds, so users can pay for what they need and afford the service they receive.	• Assume making a network available will lead to increased "civic engagement", or participation in local government.

Planning	
Success	**Failure**
• Develop a city-wide economic improvement plan that includes the network as one (but not the only) aspect.	• Roll out Internet access and assume it will magically reinvigorate the local economy without being a part of a greater plan.
• Create a solid plan to generate revenue and obtain paying customers before building the network.	• Build without a marketing and monetization plan and hope people will pay to use the network.
• Leverage the municipality's existing utility infrastructure and utility providers as a basis.	• Rely entirely on outside companies to build new infrastructure.

Political	
Success	**Failure**
• Through lobbying and activism, work with state legislators to repeal restrictive state laws.	• Assume the FCC can or will intervene to preempt restrictive state laws.
• Appeal to community spirit, not partisan politics, to introduce legislation that makes municipal networks possible.	• Frame the municipal broadband debate as a partisan issue.
• Be prepared to reorganize network ownership to comply with state regulatory environments.	• Treat network development as a one-size-fits-all solution without considering the local legal environment.

Technology	
Success	**Failure**
• Build fiber for the future, and supplement it with wireless access as needed in regions not yet reached by the main fiber network, and in areas such as parks where monetizing access is less achievable.	• Decide against building fiber because of the higher short-term costs to build. Instead, attempt to blanket a municipality with less expensive wireless technologies.
• Plan to expand a fiber-based network to meet future increases in connectivity demands, building developments, and urban expansion.	• Hand out free Wi-Fi access to downtown areas and urban centers, and assume that economic revitalization will magically happen on its own.
• Build a fiber network that offers superior speed and reliability than private competitors currently provide to the municipality.	• Assume that current state-of-the-art wireless networks will not be made obsolete by technological advances in the near future.

Finance	
Success	**Failure**
• Issue bonds or use interdepartmental loans to fund municipal broadband projects without taxation.	• Try to fund a network by raising taxes or dipping into a tax revenue stream.
• Apply for federal stimulus funds in the form of grants and loans where communities qualify for them.	• Assume the federal government will be of no help simply because of the current position of the FCC's leadership or presidential administration.
• In a financial analysis, include subsequent reductions in expenses and increases in revenue the municipality will gain.	• Treat the cost to build the network as the only relevant financial dimension, and ignore the long-term expense reductions of the public's owning its own network.
• Make the public sector its own ISP, thereby reducing costs and improving service.	• Assume advertising and residential service subscriptions will recoup the initial investment.

Business Model	
Success	**Failure**
• Maintain municipal ownership and control of the network instead of farming it out to private, profit-driven companies.	• Take a "hands-off" approach to letting a private company build, manage, and monetize the network. Ignore the reality that private companies are routinely restructured, sold, put out of business, or change their operational focus.
• Create realistic financial plans that produce predictable profits for private partners, including leasing and reselling network access.	• Choose a financially unstable private partner in hopes the network's profits will stabilize them.

VII. CONCLUSION.

The political dimension of municipal broadband largely defines whether such networks are legally possible to build in any given state. But it takes more than favorable legislation to make a network successful. Public administrators must also consider other dimensions of the problem: social, technological, financial, planning, and business models.

This multi-faceted problem does have solutions, and local governments across the nation have risen to the challenge of finding them. By learning from past triumphs and tragedies, administrators of future projects can steer projects in the right direction from the very beginning. Although the status of Internet access as a public utility remains contested at the federal level, delivering it as such has become a reality for hundreds of municipalities in the United States.

In Arizona, several cities and tribal regions have created and expanded their network infrastructures to spur economic development and connect underserved areas to the world-wide web. Yet in the ever-shifting winds of public policy, citizens must keep a watchful eye on their state legislatures and their representatives in Congress, because private cable companies and ISPs continue to bring self-serving and restrictive bills to politicians at all levels of government.

Municipalities can revitalize their communities

and improve their finances by taking the future of broadband into their own hands. Will federal courts and regulatory agencies help them or hinder them in this endeavor?

That remains to be seen.

FOOTNOTES

[1] See "Community Network Map", from Community Networks: A Project of the Institute for Local Self-Reliance. https://muninetworks.org/communitymap

[2] ILSR Fact Sheet "How Municipal Networks are Financed", p. 1. https://ilsr.org/wp-content/uploads/2014/01/financing-munis-fact-sheet.pdf

[3] ILSR Fact Sheet, "Community Broadband Creates Public Savings", p. 1–2. https://ilsr.org/wp-content/uploads/2012/11/fact-sheet-public-finance.pdf

REFERENCES

ACC (Arizona Corporation Commission). (February 16, 2017). "Regulated Electric Utilities List". http://www.azcc.gov/Divisions/Utilities/Utility_List/electric.pdf

See also the ACC's "Utilities Division" page on "Electric": http://www.azcc.gov/divisions/utilities/electric.asp

ACC (Arizona Corporation Commission). (2017). "Who Regulates Salt River Project (SRP)". http://www.azcc.gov/divisions/utilities/electric/srp.asp

Albanesius, Chloe. (December 21, 2009). "Philadelphia

Repurchases City Wi-Fi Network for $2M". *PCMag.* https://www.pcmag.com/article2/0,2817,2357395,00.a sp

Bain, Brian, and Rock, Brian. (2011). "A Survey of the 802.11 IEEE Standard and Its Practical Applications". Survey paper on file at Ohio State University as part of the course *CSE 679: Introduction to Multimedia Networking (Autumn 2011).* http://web.cse.ohio-state.edu/~xuan.3/courses/679/topic_4a_rep.pdf

Baller, James. (June 2014). "State Restrictions on Community Broadband Services or Other Public Communications Initiatives (as of June 1, 2014)". *The Baller Herbst Law Group.* https://ecfsapi.fcc.gov/file/7521826169.pdf

Bode, Karl. (October 24, 2017). "Michigan Lawmaker Flees Twitter After Reports Highlight She Helped AT&T Push Anti-Competition Broadband Law". *TechDirt.* https://www.techdirt.com/articles/20171023/11391838 461/michigan-lawmaker-flees-twitter-after-reports-highlight-she-helped-att-push-anti-competition-broadband-law.shtml

BroadbandNow. (2017). "SRP Telecom Availability & Coverage Map". *Microbrand Media LLC.* https://broadbandnow.com/Salt-River-Project

Carter, Jeremy G.; Grommon, Eric. (September, 2014). "Wireless Broadband for Municipal Police: Evaluating Clearance Times of Calls for Service". *Police Quarterly, (17)3:* 226-249. DOI: 10.1177/1098611114533553.

http://journals.sagepub.com.ezproxy.fhsu.edu:2048/
doi/pdf/10.1177/1098611114533553

City of Tempe, AZ. (2017). "Public WiFi Terms of
Service". *Tempe.gov*. http://www.tempe.gov/city-
hall/communication-and-media-relations/wifi-
terms-of-service

DeCarlo, Scott, editor. (2016). "Fortune Global 500."
Fortune. http://beta.fortune.com/global500/verizon-
30

Dunne, Matthew. (June 2007). "Let My People Go
(Online): The Power of the FCC to Preempt State
Laws That Prohibit Municipal Broadband". *Columbia
Law Review, (107)*5: 1126-1163.

Dingwall, Craig. (December 2006). "Municipal
Broadband: Challenges and Perspectives". *Federal
Communications Law Journal, (59)*1: 67-102. 36p.

FCC (Federal Communications Commission). (2017).
"Commissioner Mignon Clyburn".
https://www.fcc.gov/general/commissioner-mignon-
clyburn

Ford, George S.; Koutsky, Thomas M. (November 2005).
"Broadband and Econonomic Development: A
Municipal Case Study from Florida". *Review of Urban
& Regional Development Studies, (17)*3: 216-229.
DOI: 10.1111/j.1467-940X.2005.00107.x.

Gila River Telecommunications, Inc. (2017). "Telephone
and Internet Services".
http://www.gilarivertel.com/residential/telephone

Gonzalez, Lisa. (February 26, 2015). "Transcript: Community Broadband Bits, Episode 139". Interview with Alex Deshuk, Manager of Technology and Innovation for Mesa. *Community Networks, a project of the ILSR.* https://muninetworks.org/content/transcript-community-broadband-bits-episode-139

Gonzalez, Lisa. (February 16, 2016). "South Central Communications Bringing Fiber to Members in Utah, Arizona". *Community Networks, a project of the ILSR.* https://muninetworks.org/content/south-central-communications-bringing-fiber-members-utah-arizona

Gonzalez, Lisa. (March 4, 2017). "TN Sen. Bolling Explains Her Proposal: Share This Video". *Community Networks, a project of the ILSR.* https://muninetworks.org/content/tn-sen-bolling-explains-her-proposal-share-video

Gonzalez, Lisa. (March 23, 2017). "Legislative Relief for Pinetops in Sight". *Community Networks, a project of the ILSR.* https://muninetworks.org/content/legislative-relief-pinetops-sight

Gross, Grant. (February 26, 2015). "FCC votes to overturn state laws limiting municipal broadband". *IDG Communications, Inc.: CIO.com.* http://www.cio.com/article/2889633/fcc-votes-to-overturn-state-laws-limiting-municipal-broadband.html

Hansen, Kristena. (March 6, 2011). "New online world

ahead for Indian reservations". *The Arizona Republic*. http://archive.azcentral.com/arizonarepublic/news/articles/20110306indian-reservations-online-world.html

Harris, Blake. (December 1, 2006). "Tempe, Arizona: First U.S. Citywide Public Access Wi-Fi". *GovTech*. http://www.govtech.com/dc/articles/Tempe-Arizona-First-US-Citywide-Public.html

Howard, Matthew. (December 5, 2015). *Net Neutrality for Broadband: Understanding the FCC's 2015 Open Internet Order*. Phoenix, AZ: Puma Concolor Aeternus Press.

Howard, Matthew. (February 2017). *Two Years with Net Neutrality: A Policy Analysis Follow-Up*. Phoenix, AZ: Puma Concolor Aeternus Press. Available in the current edition of *Net Neutrality for Broadband: Understanding the FCC's 2015 Open Internet Order*.

Hsieh, Po-An , et. al. (July–September 2012). "The Bumpy Road to Universal Access: An Actor-Network Analysis of a U.S. Municipal Broadband Internet Initiative". *The Information Society, (28)4*: 264–283. DOI: 10.1080/01972243.2012.689271

Hu, Jim. (February 28, 2005). "Why our broadband policy's still a mess". *ZDNet*. http://www.zdnet.com/article/why-our-broadband-policys-still-a-mess-5000141491/

Community Networks, a Project of the Institute for Local Self-Reliance (ILSR). (February 24, 2015). "Mesa's Focus on Dig Once and Fiber Leases Pays Off —

Community Broadband Buts Podcast 139."
https://muninetworks.org/content/mesas-focus-dig-
once-and-fiber-leases-pays-community-broadband-
bits-podcast-139

Kang, Cecelia. (August 26, 2016). "Broadband Law Could
Force Rural Residents Off Information
Superhighway". *Technology, The New York Times.*
https://www.nytimes.com/2016/08/29/technology/br
oadband-law-could-force-rural-residents-off-
information-superhighway.html

Kidd, Dorothy. (January 2009). "Much more than a little
byte: citizens and broadband". *International Journal
of Media and Cultural Politics, (5)1/2: 7-21.*
DOI: 10.1386/macp.5.1-2.7_1.

King, Joe. (Summer 2014). "Connecting Danville, Virginia
to the Future". *Economic Development Journal, (13)3:*
35-42.

Lawson, Stephen. (December 12, 2007). "Tempe Wi-Fi
network on the block". *PC World.*
http://www.washingtonpost.com/wp-
dyn/content/article/2007/12/12/AR2007121201073.htm
l

Lefler, Dion. (May 24, 2014). "Chanute aims to provide
speedy Internet service to all homes, businesses in
town." *Wichita Eagle.*
http://www.kansas.com/news/article1144149.html

Leibowitz, Jon. (September 22, 2005). "Municipal
Broadband: Should Cities Have a Voice?" *Remarks to
the 25th Annual Conference of the National*

Association of Telecommunications Officers and Advisors (NATOA).
https://www.ftc.gov/sites/default/files/documents/public_statements/municipal-broadband-should-cities-have-voice/050922municipalbroadband.pdf

Nuechterlein, Jonathan E., and Weiser, Philip J. (2013). *Digital Crossroads: Telecommunications Law and Policy in the Internet Age, 2nd Edition.* Cambridge, MA: MIT Press.

Mandviwalla, Munir, et. al. (February 2008). "Municipal Broadband Wireless Networks". *Communications of the ACM, (51)*2: 72-80.
DOI: 10.1145/1314215.1314228.

O'Rielly, Michael. (January 30, 2015). "Municipal Broadband: A Snapshot". *Federal Communications Commission (FCC).*
https://www.fcc.gov/news-events/blog/2015/01/30/municipal-broadband-snapshot

Park, Namkee, and Lee, Kwan Min. (2010). "Wireless Cities: Local Governments' Involvement in the Shaping of Wi-Fi Networks". *Journal of Broadcasting & Electronic Media,* 54(3): 425–442. DOI: 10.1080/08838151.2010.498849
http://mc7290.bgsu.wikispaces.net/file/view/Park+%26+Lee.pdf

Reuters. (August 10, 2016). "U.S. Court Blocks FCC Bid to Expand Public Broadband". *Technology, The New York Times. NYTimes*.com.
https://www.nytimes.com/2016/08/10/technology/10r

euters-usa-internet-ruling.html

Settles, Craig. (July 20, 2014). "Mr. Wheeler, tear down these walls: The economic case for removing barriers to muni broadband". *GigaOm.com.* https://gigaom.com/2014/07/20/mr-wheeler-tear-down-these-walls-the-economic-case-for-removing-barriers-to-muni-broadband/

Stewart, Matt. (February 17, 2014). "Cable bill proposal in Kansas causes controversy in Kansas City". *Fox4KC: Fox News.* http://fox4kc.com/2014/02/17/cable-bill-proposal-in-kansas-causes-controversy-in-kansas-city/

Tapia, Andrea H., and Ortiz, Julio Angel. (February 2010). "Network Hopes: Municipalities Deploying Wireless Internet to Increase Civic Engagement". *Social Science Computer Review, (28)*1: 93-117.

Teters, Christopher. (December 18, 2015). "Municipal Broadband in Kansas: The Fight for Community Manifest Destiny". *Kansas Journal of Law & Public Policy, (25)*1: 89-110.

Vos, Esme. (September 28, 2009). "St. Cloud shuts down free citywide WiFi service". *MuniWireless.* http://muniwireless.com/2009/09/28/st-cloud-shuts-down-free-citywide-wifi-service/

Vos, Esme. (May 31, 2011). "Court awards Tempe $1.8M, ownership of citywide WiFi network". *MuniWireless.* http://muniwireless.com/2011/05/31/court-awards-tempe-ownership-of-citywide-wifi-network/

Wyatt, Edward. (February 3, 2014). "Fast Internet Is Chattanooga's New Locomotive". *The New York Times*. https://www.nytimes.com/2014/02/04/technology/fast-internet-service-speeds-business-development-in-chattanooga.html

APPENDIX
FIBER NETWORKS: AN ABBREVIATION GUIDE.

Fiber optic cable provides faster transmission than the copper wires which historically comprise traditional telephone networks. Many residential and business locations still depend on copper wire to connect to the Internet.

FTTN (Fiber to the Node) refers to locations connected to a fiber network via copper wires. Because of the copper wire, these locations have limited bandwidth (and therefore, connection speed) that does not realize the full potential of an entirely fiber network.

Eliminating copper to connect the fiber directly to each location achieves maximum connection speed. This completely fiber network is called **FTTP (Fiber to the Premises)** or sometimes **FTTH (Fiber to the Home)**.

FTTN infrastructure typically costs less to build, and can achieve useful bandwidth.

FTTP infrastructure has greater costs to build, and so remains less frequently used in the USA despite its potential for significantly greater speed.

Fiber Backhaul: Backhaul means the parts of a network connecting the core (or backbone) network to the subnetworks at the edge.

A more detailed comparison of fiber networks and their underlying technology can be found in: Nuechterlein, Jonathan E., and Weiser, Philip J. (2013). *Digital Crossroads: Telecommunications Law and Policy in the Internet Age, 2nd Edition*, pp. 25–28 and 71–74.

MORE POLICY BOOKS FROM
MATTHEW HOWARD

Laws That Shape Our Lives: Public Policy Essays

The Problems of Political Appointees in Federal Government: Causes, Effects, and Solutions

Net Neutrality for Broadband: Understanding the FCC's 2015 Open Internet Order (Current edition includes the follow-up, *Two Years with Net Neutrality*).

Tobacco and Fluoride: Two Essays on Domestic and International Public Health Policy.

Patents and Public Health: Two Essays on Medicine & Genetics as Intellectual Property.

For a complete list of paperbacks and ebooks currently in print, please see:

http://Author.to/MatthewHoward